If My Mom Were A Platypus

If My Mom Were A Platypus

ANIMAL BABIES
AND THEIR MOTHERS

BY Dia L. Michels

ILLUSTRATIONS BY Andrew Barthelmes

Platypus Media LLC
Washington DC, USA
2001

For Akaela, Zaydek and Miralah —my animal babies

Library of Congress Cataloging-in-Publication Data

Michels, Dia L.
  If my mom were a platypus: animal babies and their
mothers / by Dia L. Michels; illustrations by Andrew Barthelmes.– 1st
ed.
      p. cm.
  ISBN 1-930775-02-4 (alk. paper)
1. Mammals—Infancy—Juvenile literature. [1. Mammals—Infancy. 2.
Animals—Infancy. 3. Mother and child.] I. Barthelmes, Andrew, ill. II.
Title.
  QL706.2 .M53 2001
  599.13'9—dc21

                        2001000614

Text and Illustrations © 2001 Platypus Media LLC
All rights reserved
Published by Platypus Media LLC
627 A Street, NE
Washington, DC 20002 USA
PlatypusMedia.com
ISBN: 1-930775-02-4
Printed in the United States of America

10 9 8 7 6 5 4 3 2 1

Activity guide available at PlatypusMedia.com

EDITORIAL: Ellen E.M. Roberts, Where Books Begin, New York, NY
RESEARCH DIRECTOR: Emily Schuster, Silver Spring, MD
RESEARCH ASSOCIATE: Judith Schaefer, Washington, DC
DESIGN: Nina Barnett, New York, NY
CREATIVE DIRECTION: Douglas Wink, Inkway Graphics, Jersey City, NJ
PRODUCTION: Millicent Fairhurst, MF Book Production Services, New York, NY

Table of Contents

Platypus 7

Ⓔ African Elephant 11

Ⓔ Koala 15

Ⓔ Golden Lion Tamarin Monkey 19

Ⓔ Pacific Gray Whale 22

Ⓔ Giraffe 27

Least Shrew 31

Ⓔ Hooded Seal 35

Mexican Free-Tailed Bat 39

Lion 42

Ⓔ Polar Bear 47

Hippopotamus 51

Ⓔ Orangutan 54

Human 59

Glossary 62

Index 64

Many mammals are today in danger of disappearing from our earth. The symbol E within a circle indicates these animals.

If my mom were a Platypus . . .

. . . I would have hatched from an egg!

How Were You Born?

To get ready for me, my mom built a nest beside a stream. In it she laid two leathery eggs the size of grapes. Platypus babies usually come in pairs. Our two eggs were stuck together so we wouldn't roll around. My mom scooped the eggs up with her tail and placed them on her belly. We rested there for ten days until hatching time.

I was bean-sized, bright pink, and hairless when I hatched with my eyes sealed shut. I clung to my mom's fur. Milk began to ooze out from the milk patches on her chest. I lapped the milk up from her fur.

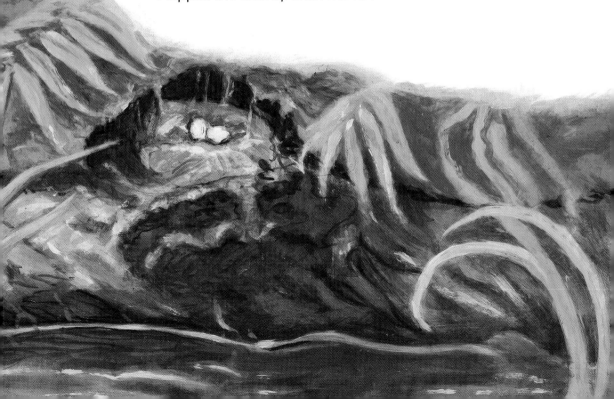

How Did You Grow?

For nearly four months, I lived on my mom's milk. As I grew, my brown fur came in soft and silky. My eyes opened and I could crawl, growl like a puppy, and make kissing sounds. When my mom left the nest to get food for herself, she always plugged the entrance with mud so my twin and I would be safely hidden. Each time she returned she had to dig her way back into the nest.

What Do You Know?

Now I am four months old. Today I am leaving the nest for the first time. I am over a foot long and weigh about one pound. My mom leads me into the water for my first swim. She shows me how to catch insect eggs, which she crushes between two hard plates in her jaws for me to eat.

For the first month, I return to my nest to sleep with my mom. After that, I will leave to dig my own tunnel in another stream. Here I will make a nest for my own babies someday.

8

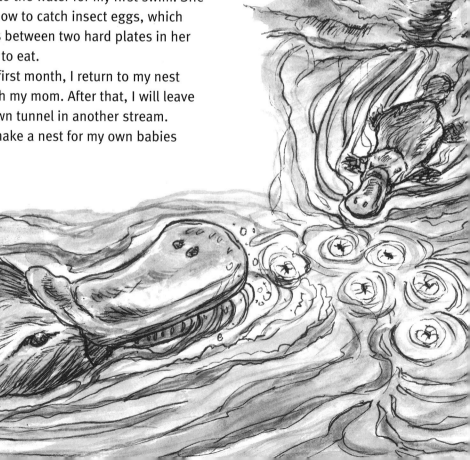

And What Do You Eat?

I look on the bottom of the stream for food.
With my bill I find creatures to eat, like
shrimp and worms. My bill helps me find
food I can't see. It is soft and flexible, not
hard like a duck's bill. I curl my bill into a flat
tube that I use to suck in the shrimp and
worms. I keep them in my cheek pouches
until I get back up to the surface of the
stream. I grind my food in my jaws while I
float in the water.

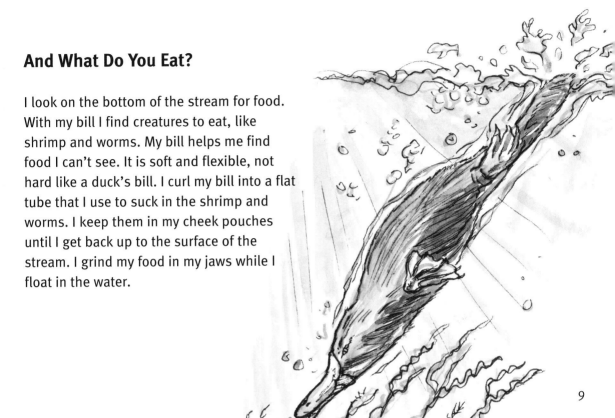

9

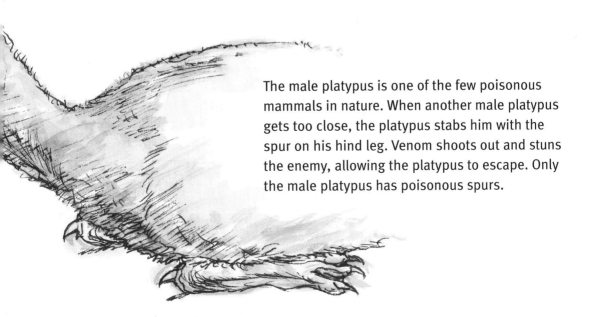

The male platypus is one of the few poisonous
mammals in nature. When another male platypus
gets too close, the platypus stabs him with the
spur on his hind leg. Venom shoots out and stuns
the enemy, allowing the platypus to escape. Only
the male platypus has poisonous spurs.

If my mom were an African Elephant . . .

. . . I would have been born with a big thump!

How Were You Born?

After nearly two years inside my mom, I was ready to be born. My mom moved close to another female elephant, steadying herself against her broad warm back. Then the other elephant cows and calves gathered round, rumbling loudly, waving their trunks, and flapping their ears. I dropped to the ground from between my mom's hind legs with a big thump.

Using their trunks, tusks, and front feet, my mom and the other elephant cleaned me up. In less than twenty minutes I was standing on wobbly legs. My mom powdered me with huge clouds of dust to help dry me off. Then she slipped away for a drink. The other elephants took care of me until my mom came back.

How Did You Grow?

I was born big—about three feet tall and over two hundred pounds—just the right size for a baby elephant. When my mom was standing or walking, I fit right underneath her. I let my trunk hang down limply to one side and reached up with my lips to a nipple between my mom's front legs. I nursed for a minute or two every half-hour. Sometimes I sucked my trunk just like a human baby sucking on his thumb.

Elephants grow up slowly. Until I am nine, I will spend at least half my time very close to my mom. A male elephant leaves his family group when he is between twelve and twenty years old. A female stays with the family her whole life.

What Do You Know?

My family teaches me things elephants need to know: how to recognize each other, how to find food and water, and how to swim using my trunk like a snorkel. As I learn, my mom takes good care of me. If I wander off, she comes after me. If I stumble, she wraps her trunk around my body and helps me to my feet. She helps me up hills and over fallen logs. She boosts me out of deep mud. She nudges and comforts me with her trunk. Sometimes, if I misbehave, she slaps me with it. The best thing she does with it is wash me!

We always travel with our herd of other elephant cows and calves. My father and the other bull elephants usually only join us when it is time to mate.

And What Do You Eat?

My first teeth were only the size of quarters, not big enough to chew the tough leaves and grasses that elephants like. For the first three months of my life, my mom's milk was my only food.

I lose my baby teeth and grow larger new teeth so that I can eat plants. I will nurse until I am over four years old and have tusks twelve inches long. By then I will find all of my own food. Then I will use my trunk to pick plants growing on the ground or high in the trees. I will spend sixteen hours a day looking for food.

Elephant feet are tough enough for walking over rocks and stones, but they're also soft and spongy. Big, round feet help spread an elephant's weight over a large area. This takes the pressure of all that weight off the leg bones. With these big, soft padded feet, elephants can move quietly, even though they can grow to weigh more than five tons. Elephants barely ever leave footprints.

If my mom were a Koala . . .

. . . I would have been born in a tree in Australia!

How Were You Born?

Before I was born, mom already had a nest for me. Not a nest like a bird makes, but a soft, warm pouch on her belly. She sat in the branches of a eucalyptus tree and waited. The fur on her bottom was a fine, soft cushion. Finally, out I came—smaller than a grape! My eyes and ears were sealed shut. You could see my blood vessels through my thin skin.

I had tiny, needle-sharp claws on my front feet and strong shoulder muscles. I could crawl through my mom's thick fur to the small, round opening of her pouch. Her pouch opens backward, toward her feet, unlike a kangaroo's pouch. Once inside, I found two nipples. I latched on to one. It swelled so that I couldn't possibly fall off. I stayed there for six months drinking my mom's milk.

How Did You Grow?

Slowly, I began to grow as I drank my mom's milk. Her pouch stretched and grew with me. When my eyes finally opened, I peeped out for the first time. I was a scrawny little thing with short, flat, brown fur.

When I began leaving my mom's pouch for little outings, I smelled something good to eat nearby. I stretched my head until I found a soft, dark greenish substance, called pap, coming out of my mom's anus. It was made of leaves that my mom had chewed and swallowed.

As I began eating pap, my mom's milk became thicker and richer. Feeding on milk and pap, I grew fast. Within two weeks my teeth came in and I became the fluffy, furry koala that I am today.

16

What Do You Know?

I began leaving the pouch to play around on my mom's body. By the time I was seven months old, I had outgrown the pouch and stopped breastfeeding. Now I curl up on my mom's lap to sleep. When I wake up I ride on her back as she moves from one clump of eucalyptus leaves to another.

By my first birthday my mom will be expecting a new joey. When he pokes his head out of her pouch, I will have to leave my mom. There won't be enough good leaves in her patch of trees to support all of us, so I'll have to go out and find a tree of my very own.

And What Do You Eat?

We koalas have a slow, lazy life. We sleep all day in our tree. Then at night we eat our favorite food—eucalyptus leaves. They contain plenty of water so I don't need to drink very much. I like eucalyptus leaves so much that I can stay in the same tree for days at a time. I eat box leaves and mistletoe too.

Eucalyptus is used to make cough drops—and because koalas eat so much eucalyptus, they smell like cough drops, too! The smell helps them keep fleas away. There are more than seven hundred kinds of eucalyptus trees in Australia, but koalas eat leaves from only fifteen of them. Their noses help them sniff out the right kind of eucalyptus leaves.

If my mom were a Golden Lion Tamarin Monkey...

...I would have been born in the family bed!

How Were You Born?

My mom gave birth to me, one of two tamarin twins, in a hole in a tree. My family had used this nest for so long that it was cushioned by a thick layer of tamarin fur. We all slept huddled together, enjoying each other's warmth, companionship, and smell.

I was born on a rainy spring night. My beady black eyes were wide open. I was three inches long, with a two-inch tail, and a golden fur coat. I only weighed one ounce. I was no bigger than my dad's head. Though young, I was already an expert at three life-saving skills: clinging, crawling, and sucking. With slender, long-clawed fingers and toes I clung to my mom's fur. I climbed up through it to find her nipples, one for me and one for my twin.

How Did You Grow?

For the first two weeks, I had to be carried all day long. My father and my older brothers and sisters all took turns carrying me. At first, I never left my mom's body unless I was snatched away. My instinct for clinging was strong, but sometimes one of the other monkeys in the nest would pull me off her back. My mom might scrape me off against a branch, squeaking and nipping at me. She wasn't trying to hurt me. When my mom needed to look for food, she might push me off her back by rubbing against a branch. She could find food more easily without me.

By my third week, my mom was still feeding me, but my father was now carrying me most of the time. Two weeks later, I was big enough to start running, jumping, and climbing on my own. Soon my family didn't have to carry me anymore. I stopped breast-feeding, too.

What Do You Know?

My twin and I play a lot. We wrestle, grapple, pounce, and chase. Hide-and-seek is one of our favorite games. So is catapult: I lean on branches to bend them and they send me flying as they spring back into shape. Sometimes my twin and I both pounce on one of the adults. Usually our play is just fun, but if we make too much of a ruckus, an adult might punish the one who starts it.

And What Do You Eat?

Lion tamarin monkeys share their food. When I was five weeks old, I started eating solid food. Whoever was carrying me would pass back soft fruit or a juicy worm. Now that my first teeth have come in, I can enjoy crunchy grasshoppers and cockroaches, too.

I scamper about with the rest of my family as they eat and rest in our nesting hole. When I am a year-and-a-half old, I will leave home to start my own family.

21

Tamarins may have two sets of twins a year. There are always infants around, so it takes the whole family to raise them. A young tamarin will start to baby-sit for his younger brothers and sisters not long after he stops nursing himself. If there's a choice, moms and sisters would rather carry female babies and fathers and brothers would rather carry males.

If my mom were a Pacific Gray Whale . . .

. . . I would have been born underwater!

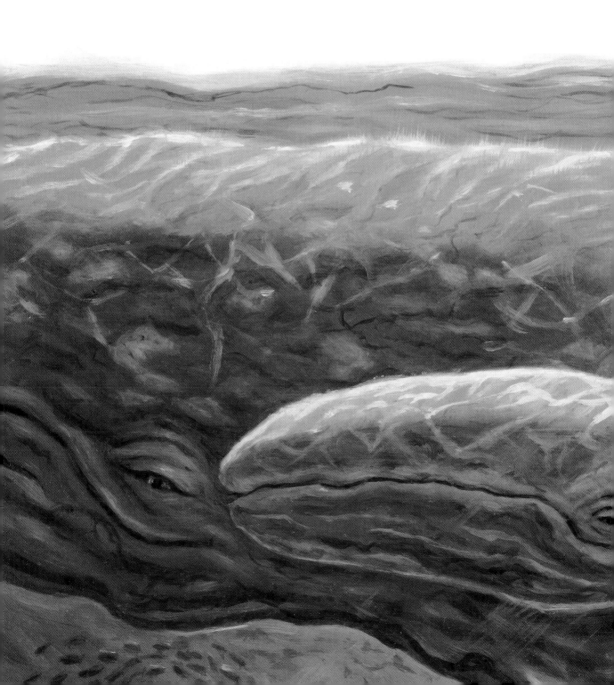

How Were You Born?

Before I was born, my mom spent the summer off the coast of Alaska. Big as a school bus and weighing thirty tons, she ate nine hundred pounds of worms, crabs, and shrimp-like krill every day to get ready for a long trip south. There wouldn't be anything to eat along the way. The pad of blubber under my mom's skin would keep her—and me, still inside her—alive and warm.

Swimming slowly, my mom and other pregnant female whales spend about three months at sea. They travel five thousand miles to lagoons off the coast of Mexico. Our journey is the longest-known migration of any mammal. Finally, my mom heads for the shallowest water where I squirm out, tail first, into the water. Three hours later, I can float by myself and swim a straight course.

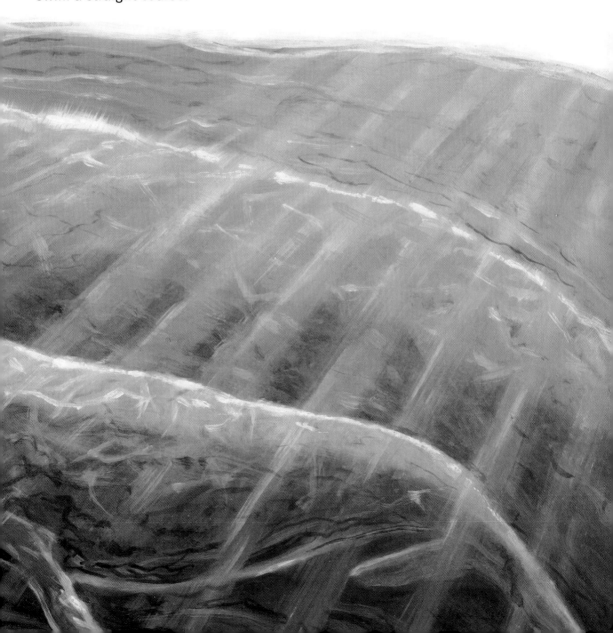

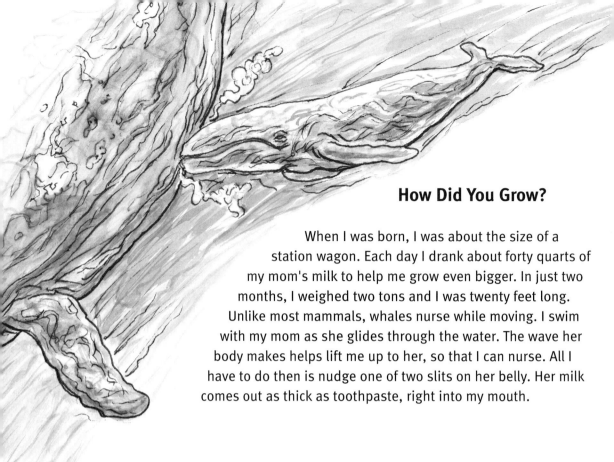

How Did You Grow?

When I was born, I was about the size of a station wagon. Each day I drank about forty quarts of my mom's milk to help me grow even bigger. In just two months, I weighed two tons and I was twenty feet long. Unlike most mammals, whales nurse while moving. I swim with my mom as she glides through the water. The wave her body makes helps lift me up to her, so that I can nurse. All I have to do then is nudge one of two slits on her belly. Her milk comes out as thick as toothpaste, right into my mouth.

What Do You Know?

During my first two months, I stay close to my mom's side. If a killer whale approaches, my mom defends me. There are other moms and calves nearby, but my mom and I stay by ourselves.

The warm water is lovely, but we need food, so Mom and I begin the journey north. I am still nursing, so I'm not hungry yet. I have even grown my own pad of blubber. We will reach our Arctic feeding grounds in June. I will keep nursing for another couple of months. By that time, my mom will have given me six thousand quarts of milk. I will be ready to start eating worms and crabs of my own.

And What Do You Eat?

Gray whales have yellow bristles called baleen inside their mouths instead of teeth. The baleen works like a sieve, straining out the mud when I look for food. I swim along the ocean bottom, sucking up mud to get the small animals that live in it like worms and tiny fish called krill. I let the mud and water strain out and eat the worms and krill.

After their babies are born, most mammal moms lean down and break the umbilical cord with their teeth. Whales can't do that because they can't bend that far. Instead, they spin while giving birth, steering with their flippers. This spinning causes tension that helps the umbilical cord to snap.

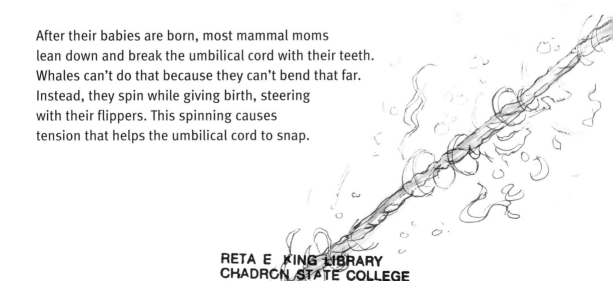

If my mom were a Giraffe . . .

. . . I would have been born into thin air!

How Were You Born?

When it was time for my birth, my mom headed away from the other giraffes. She walked over to the place in our home range where giraffes are born. It is called the calving ground. I was born front feet first, with my little head between my legs. I fell about five feet from my mom to the ground.

My mom licked me all over with her long, rough tongue paying special attention to my eyes, nose, and ears. My short coat, already patterned with brown blotches, was soft and woolly. My hooves were soft, but they hardened quickly. Within the hour, I could stand on them. I began to suck on one of my mom's four nipples. I was six feet tall and weighed one hundred and fifty pounds that first day.

How Did You Grow?

Many mammals spend their childhood running, jumping, and playing, but giraffe babies play less because we need to use our energy to grow. I spent my days resting with other calves my age. We touched and licked noses to get to know each other. I ran around sometimes, but I spent most of my first three months just lying or standing around, scratching the ground, and licking my coat. A giraffe protects herself by being big, so I needed to grow as large as I could, as fast as I could. I grew over three feet in six months. Now I am nine feet tall!

What Do You Know?

During the day, my mom goes away to eat. Thirteen feet tall, with large, sharp eyes, she can see for miles around. If danger threatens, she will return quickly. She can kick predators with her long legs and hard, sharp hooves. Usually I am safe because most giraffe predators such as lions, leopards, hyenas, and wild dogs feed at night when my mom is by my side. Giraffes band together in very loose herds. There are always giraffes drifting in and out of my herd. Adult giraffes spend less than an hour a day associating with each other and usually stay sixty feet apart. We are very quiet animals, but baby giraffes can bleat. Adults can snort and roar.

And What Do You Eat?

Now that I am six months old, I have started following my mom as she feeds. She shows me how to strip the leaves off acacia trees with my long, flexible tongue.

Drinking water is hard—I have to bend my legs and then lower my neck to drink. It would be easy for a lion to attack me in this awkward position. Luckily, I can go for weeks without drinking because I get most of my water from leaves.

Toward the end of my first year, I will eat more leaves and nurse less. Just after my first birthday, I will stop nursing entirely. I will stay near my mom for another two months before beginning life on my own.

Giraffes have such long necks they can eat leaves that are high up in the trees. The tallest giraffes can eat leaves that grow nineteen feet above ground! A giraffe's neck has only seven bones in it—the same number humans and most other mammals have. The bones can be up to a foot long and they are supported by very strong muscles.

If my mom were a Least Shrew . . .

. . . I would have been born to hustle!

How Were You Born?

Almost everything in a least shrew's life happens at top
speed. My mom scurried about with bits of dried grass,
leaves, and moss in her mouth to build a nest for me. With
her long, pointed snout, she wove the strands into a round
nest slightly smaller than a tennis ball, with little openings
for going in and out. She tumbled over and over, shaping
and hollowing it with her body.

When I was born I was the size of an almond and
weighed next to nothing. I was hairless and blind, with
blood vessels shining bright red through my thin skin and
little whiskers sticking out from my nose. On my tiny toes
were claws, perfect for climbing to a nipple to nurse. I was
one of seven babies. Bigger shrew babies push out the
smaller ones, who soon die—leaving their share of the milk
for the survivors.

How Did You Grow?

I grew up very quickly. By the end of two weeks I had grown fur and teeth. Two days later, my eyes opened. In another two days, I was almost the same size as my mom—who already had another batch of babies on the way. When I was three weeks old, I stopped nursing. I had to leave home, build my own nest, and find my own food.

32

What Do You Know?

I ran across the fields to find a place for my nest. Owls, weasels, foxes, and snakes hunt for me, but I find a spot to burrow. In the spring I will have babies of my own. Like my mom, I will build a nest for them of grass and leaves. I will search for enough insects and worms to eat to keep myself alive and produce breast-milk for my babies.

And What Do You Eat?

Least shrews are so small and have so little body fat that they need to eat every two hours. Day and night, summer and winter, I run through burrows and grass tunnels, sniffing for food. Since I don't sleep at night, I only take short naps between meals around the clock. I eat insects, centipedes, grubs, snails, earthworms, and even small frogs. If you put all the food I ate each day in one pile, it would be bigger than I am.

Shrews use their strong teeth more than most mammals. As they get older, their teeth get worn down from cracking snail shells and crunchy insects.

33

Shrews are fierce fighters. Since they hunt for food all day and all night, they must defend their feeding grounds against other shrews. A shrew fight is something to see! Squealing and screaming, they lock on to one another and roll around, kicking and biting until one gives up. The loser takes off, with the winner nipping at her rump.

If my mom were a Hooded Seal . . .

. . . I would have been born on ice!

How Were You Born?

One dark day, my mom got out of the cold ocean. It was time for me to be born so she lay down on the ice. I appeared, still packed in a sack. I wriggled inside for a minute, broke out of the sack, and began moving around on the ice. Five minutes later, my mom rolled on her side, and I began to nurse. When I wasn't nursing, her nipples disappeared deep into my mom's fur, close to her skin so nothing stuck out of her sleek body, so well-suited to swimming.

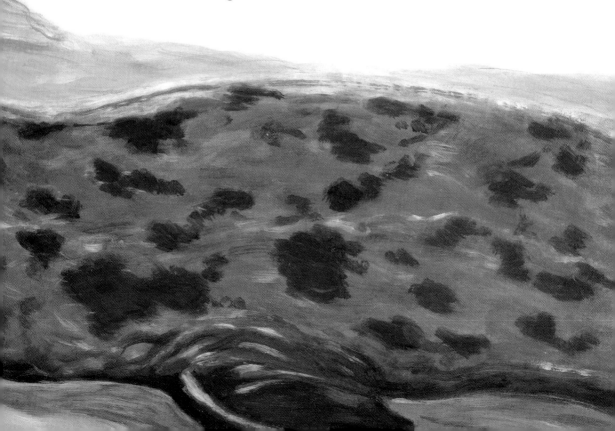

How Did You Grow?

I was three feet long and forty-four pounds when I was born. I needed to gain weight fast so my mom's body provided milk for me that was 60 percent fat, the richest milk of any mammal! I drank two gallons of the rosy-beige milk every day. In just four days my weight doubled—I wasn't a baby anymore.

My mom had never left my side—she had fed and defended me against polar bears, male seals nearly twice her size, and even humans. Just four days after I was born, she slipped off the ice and returned to the sea. She had lost weight taking care of me and had to gain it back quickly. Besides, she was already pregnant again and had to fatten up for next year's pup.

Now I am on my own.

What Do You Know?

For four weeks after my mom left me, I didn't eat a thing. I stayed by myself on the ice. In a month I lost more than a quarter of my weight. At that time, I tried going into the water. There I swam around and caught fish to eat. I spend most of my time swimming in the sea. When I'm on land, I can't move very quickly, which makes me an easy target for predators. Seals only come to land or ice to mate or to give birth to their young. When seals are hurt or sick, they go onto land to rest.

And What Do You Eat?

Now that I can hunt on my own, I eat halibut, redfish, and cod. I also eat shrimp, clams, crabs, and squid.

When I dive, I close my nose and throat so I won't swallow the sea water. I swim to the surface of the water with my catch and eat it there. I don't chew my food. I swallow it whole.

Why would an animal that lives about thirty years spend only four days being an infant, the shortest nursing period of any mammal? Hooded seals live at sea, but they must give birth and nurse out of the water. The only surface available is floating ice. Pups are born in the spring when the ice is beginning to melt and break up. A sudden storm might send pieces crashing together, crushing moms and pups. Or an ice floe might split, and moms and pups could be separated. A short childhood helps avoid these perils.

If my mom were a Mexican Free-Tailed Bat . . .

. . . I would have been one in a million (or more)!

How Were You Born?

I was one of millions of free-tailed bats born in a cave in Texas. Our moms left their winter homes in Mexico to gather together in that cave. Each bat had one baby.

I came out bottom first, with my wings folded around me. I was a big baby, already one-fourth the weight of my mom, but I was blind and nearly hairless, with tiny, sharp teeth, and my hind feet and thumbs almost adult-sized.

My mom cradled me in her up-turned tail, nipped the umbilical cord, and licked me clean. Then I nursed while she gave me a thorough sniffing-over, squeaking constantly. I answered back in my high, clear voice. Although my mom would never recognize my face—bats aren't blind, but they don't see well—she learned my smell within thirty minutes. She knows my voice so well that she can always pick me out from the millions of bat pups.

How Did You Grow?

My mom flew me to the nursery part of the cave. There I hung upside down, tightly packed with all the other pups. If you pulled at one of us, you would loosen a whole cluster of babies.

I grew rapidly. In just three weeks, I was almost adult-size. In four weeks, I had grown soft, brown fur. By five weeks, my teeth had come in and my wings spread nearly a foot.

My mom came twice a day to nurse me for about twenty minutes each time. Unlike most mammals, she had nipples on the sides of her body, not on her chest. When she was ready to go, she would pull away from me. If I held on, she would drag me along until I let go.

What Do You Know?

Now that I am five weeks old, I have started to fly. Bats are the only mammals that can truly fly. At first I flew clumsily. Now I find my way using echolocation. I make squeaking sounds that echo off objects and tell me where those objects are. That way, I don't bump into anything.

A bat's wing is really a hand with sheets of skin stretched between the fingers. When I fly, I spread out my arms and fingers so the skin is stretched tight.

By moving my fingers, I can change the shape of my wings to steer. Free-tailed bats fly faster than most other bats.

And What Do You Eat?

Bats rest in caves during the day. At sundown they leave to hunt for food. Mexican free-tailed bats eat moths, but nursing moms eat flying ants to get extra nutrients they need to make milk for their babies.

As I began to fly, I learned to hunt, too. I caught few moths at first. Until I can catch what I need to live, I will live on the fat that I stored while nursing. When I am older, I will catch insects in my teeth, eating several thousand each night.

Bats hang upside-down because they can't stand right-side-up. Their leg bones are too thin to hold up their bodies. But hanging upside-down is easy for them—their claws automatically lock onto their roost. It takes absolutely no muscle power for a bat to hang on this way.

When they are ready to fly, they let go and fall ten feet, gathering enough speed to take off.

If my mom were a Lion . . .

. . . I would have been born in hiding!

How Were You Born?

I was born in Africa in a place that was sheltered by rocks and tall grasses. My mom chose this spot to protect me from the leopards, eagles, hyenas, and enemy lions who would like to eat me. I was one of four lion cubs in the litter. When I was born, I was blind, toothless, and barely able to move. My only food was milk from my mom.

How Did You Grow?

When I was born, my mom carried me around by the scruff of my neck, even though I would grow to weigh four hundred pounds! For five weeks, I stayed in the den, safely hidden. Sometimes my mom left me for a whole day to go hunting for food.

When I learned to walk, my mom led me out of the hiding place. We joined the other lionesses—my mom's sisters and cousins—and their cubs. There were also a few adult male lions in our group, called a pride.

What Do You Know?

In our pride, the moms hunt and feed together. They defend their cubs and their territory. The biggest enemies are not other kinds of animals, but other lions. Male lions want to take over our pride and females want to steal our feeding range. Lionesses live in groups to protect themselves from these other lions. Male lions help defend the pride, too, but soon enough they will eventually be driven off by other males. Lionesses are the main hunters and defenders of the pride.

And What Do You Eat?

Lions eat antelope, wildebeests, and buffalo. Adult males eat first, females eat next, cubs eat last. Meanwhile, hyenas stand nearby, watching the feast and hoping to steal some dinner.

Slowly I am learning to hunt my own food. I practice stalking and pouncing. Lion cubs can spoil hunts by running ahead or meowing. I am learning to sit patiently and watch the hunting. My mom shows me how to kill, but doesn't help me do it. For two years, I will learn how to hunt from my mom. Then, my brothers and male cousins will wander away from the pride, but we female cubs will stay. One day I will go back to the den where I was born to give birth to my own cubs.

In one pride, all the lionesses take care of all the cubs. Any lioness will nurse any cub. A napping lioness who has been hunting all night doesn't pay much attention to who is suckling on her. And because they are all so closely related, a lioness helps the family no matter which baby she nurses.

If my mom were a Polar Bear . . .

. . . I would have been born in a snow cave!

How Were You Born?

Before I was born, my mom tunneled into a snow bank to hollow out a den for me. She made a hole in the top for air. She piled snow in front, so that warm air would stay inside. She crawled in, curled up, and dozed, waiting for my sister and me to be born.

I was born with my short fur still wet. I had no fat on my body. But my mom dried me off quickly and I snuggled deep into her fur to keep warm. I couldn't see or hear, but I could smell my mom's nipple. I crawled up her body and began to nurse.

How Did You Grow?

I was born the size of a guinea pig. My mom was four hundred times bigger than I was! I grew rapidly, drinking my mom's thick, creamy milk. At first, she lay on her side to feed me. As I grew, she sat against the cave wall and cradled me in her huge, furry arms. Sometimes she rocked gently, side to side. During this first month with her cubs, my mom didn't eat anything and never left the den.

At three weeks I could hear. Then my blue eyes opened so I could see. Two weeks later, I could chew and even walk a little. At four months, I weighed twenty-five pounds. Sleek and fat, with a thick fur coat, I was ready to leave the den for the first time. Tagging along next to Mom, I would explore the world by her side for the next two-and-a-half years.

What Do You Know?

Outside the den, I follow my mom, stepping in her big footprints. When I am tired or cold, I climb onto her back. In a few weeks, my mom will lead me into the water for my first swim. Polar bears float easily and are strong swimmers. We use our huge front paws to paddle and we steer with our hind legs. We can swim as far as sixty miles a day in water so cold that most creatures would perish in it within minutes. We can even sleep at sea!

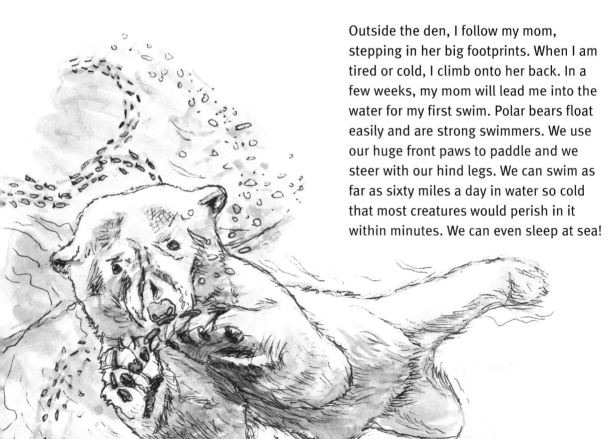

And What Do You Eat?

Polar bears eat seal meat. This is a messy business. My mom teaches me to stop every twenty minutes to go to the water and wash off the grease and blood.

When I was a year old, I began to hunt my own seal meat. At first, I didn't catch anything. It takes two years to learn to catch a seal for food.

I use my nose to track a seal for miles. I also listen for seals calling to each other underwater. Sometimes I grab a seal as he comes to the surface of the water to breathe. Other times, seals rest out on the open ice. I move toward the seal by sliding across the ice on my belly and take him by surprise.

49

A polar bear looks white, but he isn't really. The long hairs in his shaggy coat are colorless and hollow. Sunlight bounces off them and makes them appear white. The sunlight flows into each hollow hair and carries heat to the polar bear's body. Beneath his hair, the polar bear's skin is black. That helps his body absorb heat. You can see the black skin on his nose, tongue, and the soles of his feet. When the sun isn't shining, the bear's blubber keeps him warm.

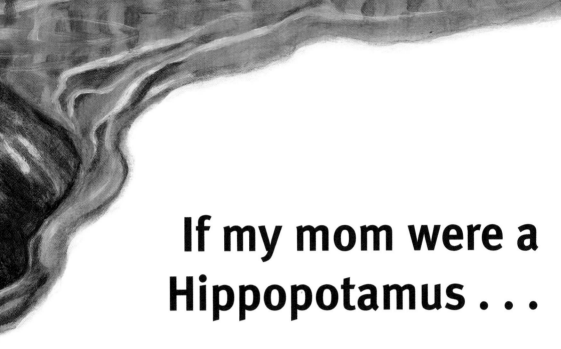

If my mom were a Hippopotamus . . .

. . . I would have been born in a crocodile-infested river!

How Were You Born?

Before I was born, my mom found a quiet spot away from the hippo herd. She lay down in water up to her eyes and nose, and out I came—first my front feet, then my head, and then my hind feet. My cradle was the warm, brown water of a slow-moving river.

Immediately, my mom poked her big head into the water and boosted me to the surface to take my first breath. Then I went back underwater to nurse. I had to fold my ears down and close my nostrils to keep the water out. Twice every minute, I bobbed to the surface to breathe and swallow.

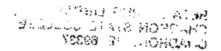

How Did You Grow?

We stayed away from the herd for two weeks, while I learned to float in the water by myself. For the first few days, my mom never left me, even to eat. She nuzzled and scraped my skin gently with her teeth. She kept me safe from hungry crocodiles—she could bite them in two with her mighty jaws. If she had to move into deeper water, she nudged me up onto her broad back to carry me.

Soon we rejoined the herd, and I continued to nurse and grow. By my first birthday, I was four times bigger than when I was born. I had stopped nursing and I had my full set of teeth. I will stay with my mom until I am five years old.

What Do You Know?

My herd spends the days in a pool in the river. Moms and calves, as well as a few males, crowd the water and the bank. Birds pick ticks from our backs. Because we are so big, we stick up out of the water. Turtles and even baby crocodiles climb aboard to lie in the sun.

During the day, I play and wrestle with other calves. Adults rest or court one another and mate. The males fight a lot—sometimes they throw water on each other, tusk-wrestle, or lunge and fall with a splash.

And What Do You Eat?

We eat grass that grows on land. Our skin
dries out quickly, though, so we can't wander
far from cooling water. Every evening at dusk,
hippos leave the water to feed. We move like
lawnmowers through the grass, cropping it close
to the ground. We always head back to the water
before the sun comes up.

 For my first five months, I stayed behind when the
adults left to feed. One female hippo stays behind to watch
the calves. Now I am strong enough to keep up with the
grazing group, walking five miles in a single file.

53

Hippos have a smelly way of sending messages to each other: they use their dung.
If moms stand up to fight a big bull hippo who is threatening their calves, he will
usually spray them all with dung. This tells the moms that he is backing off and not
to attack him. Males use this signal among themselves, too.

If my mom were an Orangutan . . .

. . . I would have been born high and dry!

How Were You Born?

About three weeks before my birth, my mom began
drinking lots of water from holes in trees. She also ate lots
of termites to get the protein she needed. She always built
nests to rest in at night, but now she began building them
during the day, too. One day, in the midst of a downpour,
she made a quick nest, seventy feet above the ground. She
gave birth to me. The nest kept us dry in the pouring rain.

I crawled into my mom's fur, holding on tightly. I
looked like my mom, but with a pink face and a silky
head with hair standing on end.

How Did You Grow?

For the next two days, my mom rested in her nest to regain her strength. Then she began to search for food. As she moved through the forest, I was always with her, clinging so tightly to the fur on her side or stomach that she didn't have to hold me. Like a bat, I was born knowing how to hang on.

I will continue to nurse, ride on her body, and sleep in her nest for more than six years. Young orangutans stay with their moms until the next infant arrives. Males begin to wander off then, but females often stay around for a while observing how babies are cared for.

What Do You Know?

I spend my days climbing, swinging, and yelling. I learn how to nurse upside-down, hanging by a hand and a foot from a branch right above my mom. Sometimes we stay with other adult females. If they have youngsters with them, I play with them. We might feed in the same tree for a day or so. Otherwise, we keep to ourselves.

For orangutans, unlike most apes, spend most of our time in trees, curving our fingers and toes like hooks over branches and vines.

And What Do You Eat?

All the while, I have been learning how to find fruit to eat. In a rain forest, fruit trees are widely scattered so keeping track of them is hard. I follow the birds like hornbills and pigeons, which spot fruits from the sky as they fly. My favorite fruit is called a durian. It has prickles on its tough skin and sweet, stinky pulp inside. Orangutans like to eat ants. Holding the back of my hand to a tree trunk, I let the ants climb over it. Then I put my hand in my mouth and nibble them off.

It rains a lot in the forest where orangutans live, so they pick large leaves or big branches to use as umbrellas. They also cover their nests to keep them dry in the rain. Every single night, orangutans just pull down leaves and branches to make new places to sleep.

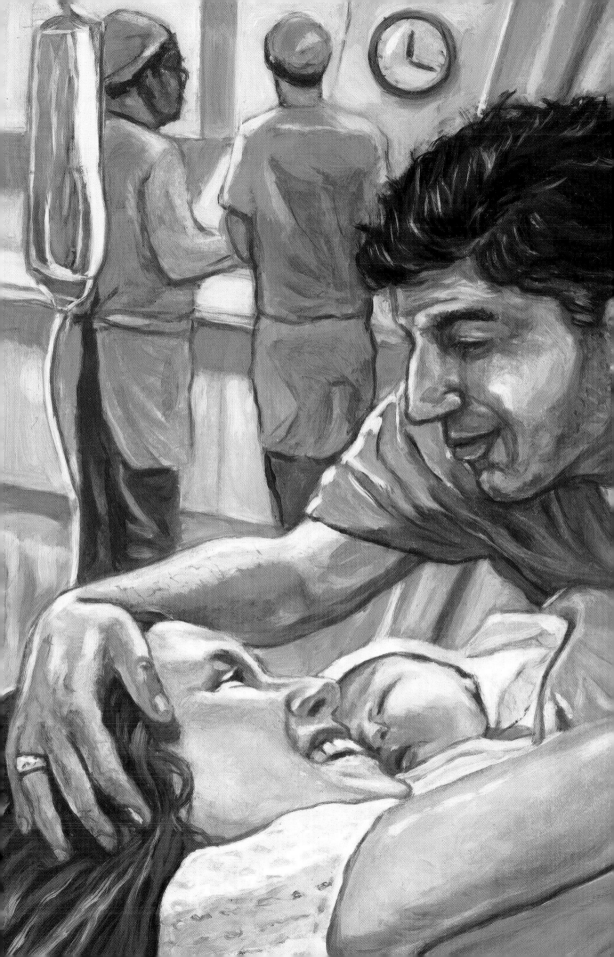

But my mom is a Human . . .

. . . and I was born in a hospital—
with a dozen people there.

How Were You Born?

After nine months inside my mom, it was time for me to be born. My mom went to a hospital where midwives, doctors, and nurses were waiting to help her. My father was at her side. A few hours after she got to the hospital, my mom gave a mighty push. I came out with my head first. After the midwife cut my umbilical cord, the nurse put a hat on my head and wrapped me in a blanket so I would be warm. She handed me to my mom to breastfeed.

The first thing I saw was my mom's face as she held me in her arms and began to nurse me. As I suckled, I held on to my mom's finger.

How Did You Grow?

My mom's breastmilk gave me everything I needed to grow
big and strong and healthy. She let me nurse whenever I was
hungry. By the time I was two weeks old, I was drinking
nearly a quart of milk a day.

I grew slowly, compared to most other mammals.
After a month, I began to smile and laugh. In the
next few months, I learned to hold up my big
heavy head and, later, to roll over. At six months,
I sat all by myself for the first time. By nine
months, I could crawl and, by my first birthday,
I had learned to walk a little.

By the time I was a few years old, I lost interest
in nursing, but I still wasn't ready to take care of
myself. Most baby mammals leave their moms and
become adults soon after they stop nursing, but human children
need their parents to watch over them long afterwards.

What Do You Know?

As I grew up, I learned about all kinds of things: how to find food, how to talk, and
how to walk. Humans have large brains. They also have hands that can do many
different movements, like pitching a ball, changing a channel, or picking up a pin.
Since humans have to learn many things in order to survive, human babies usually
stay with their parents for about twenty years.

Humans walk on just two feet, so our hands are free to do lots of things. When
I was three months old, I started to use my hands to hit at things, and three months
later, I could reach for things and grab them. Now I can use my hands to paint a
picture, put a puzzle together, or build a birdhouse.

And What Do You Eat?

At about six months, I started eating little spoonfuls of soft food, but my mom's milk was still my main meal. My teeth began to grow one after another. I had my first full set of teeth at two-and-a-half, so could eat the same food as my parents, but first they cut it into very small pieces for me.

Unlike other mammals, humans cook their food. Cooking kills germs and softens tough fibers so that humans can eat a greater variety than any other mammal.

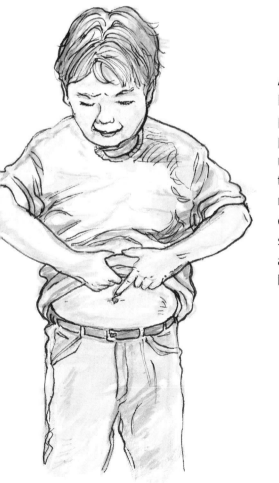

A baby grows inside her mom's uterus. The baby is connected by the umbilical cord to the placenta, the nurturing lining of the uterus. The placenta provides the baby with the oxygen and nutrients the baby needs while it grows inside the mom. Once the baby comes out of the mom, the placenta comes out too. Then the connecting umbilical cord is no longer needed, so it is cut off. It leaves a stump that falls off after a few weeks. What's left is called the belly button.

GLOSSARY

Baleen – Elastic plates of cartilage-like material that hang from the upper jaws of whales, used as a sieve to strain food from mud and water.

Blubber – The fat on marine animals from which oil is obtained.

Bull – An adult male of certain large animals, such as cattle, alligators, elephants, hippopotamuses, or moose.

Calf – The young of certain large mammals, such as elephants, whales, cows, giraffes, and hippopotamuses.

Calving Ground – Site where certain large mammals give birth.

Child – A human being between birth and puberty.

Crustaceans – Aquatic arthropods that have segmented bodies with hard outer shells, such as lobsters, crabs, krill, and barnacles.

Cub – The young of certain carnivorous animals such as the bear, wolf, or lion.

Durians – The fruit of a tree that grows in Southeast Asia. It has a hard, prickly rind and soft pulp. To humans, it has an offensive odor, but a pleasant taste.

Eucalyptus – Tall trees, native to Australia, known for their aromatic leaves.

Flipper – A wide flat limb adapted for swimming, seen in aquatic animals such as platypuses, seals, whales, and sea turtles.

Grease – Soft or melted animal fat.

Ice Floe – A large, flat expanse of floating ice.

Infant – A baby in the earliest period of life.

Joey – A baby marsupial, such as a kangaroo or a koala.

Krill – Small marine crustaceans that are the principal food of baleen whales.

Mammal – Warm-blooded vertebrate animals marked by a covering of hair on the skin and milk-producing glands in the female.

Nursing – Feeding at the breast, suckling.

Pride – A group of lions.

Primate – Any member of a mammalian order comprising apes, monkeys, and humans; includes chimpanzees, gorillas, gibbons, lemurs, and orangutans.

Pup – The young of certain animals such as dogs, wolves, foxes, bats, and seals.

Tusks – Long pointed teeth extending outside the mouth.

Umbilical Cord – The flexible cordlike structure connecting a fetus at the navel with the placenta and containing blood vessels that transport oxygen and nourishment to the fetus and remove its waste.

Wildebeest – A large bearded African antelope with curved horns.

INDEX

African Elephant 11

Alaska 23

Baleen 25

Bat *see Mexican Free-tailed Bat*

Belly button 61

Blubber 36

Breastmilk 7, 13, 16, 24, 36, 48, 60

Caves, bat 40, 41

Cheek pouches 9

Cockroaches 21

Crustacean 25

Crocodile 52

Dung, hippopotamus 53

Eggs 7

Echolocation 40

Eucalyptus Leaves 17

Elephant Feet 13

Elephant Trunk 11, 12

Elephant Tusk 11

Eyes, bat 39

Flippers 25

Footprints, polar bear 48

Giraffe 27

Golden Lion Tamarin 19

Hippopotamus 51

Herd 28

Hooded Seal 35

Hooves, Giraffe 28

Humans 59

Killer Whale 24

Koala 15

Krill 23

Least Shrew 31

Lion 42

Mexican Free-tailed Bat 39

Monkey *see Golden Lion Tamarin*

Nipples 12, 15, 19, 27, 31, 35, 47

Orangutan 54

Pacific Gray Whale 22

Platypus 7

Polar Bear 47

Pouch 16

Pride 44

Seal *see Hooded Seal*

Shrew *see Least Shrew*

Snow Cave 48

Twin Babies, Monkey 8, 19, 20, 21

Umbilical Cord 25, 39, 59

Venom 9

Whale *see Pacific Grey Whale*

Wings, bat 40